Helen Keller

Jayne Woodhouse

Heinemann
LIBRARY

First published in Great Britain by Heinemann Library
Halley Court, Jordan Hill, Oxford OX2 8EJ,
a division of Reed Educational and Professional Publishing Ltd.
Heinemann is a registered trademark of Reed Educational & Professional Publishing Limited.

OXFORD FLORENCE PRAGUE MADRID ATHENS
MELBOURNE AUCKLAND KUALA LUMPUR SINGAPORE TOKYO
IBADAN NAIROBI KAMPALA JOHANNESBURG GABORONE
PORTSMOUTH NH (USA) CHICAGO MEXICO CITY SAO PAULO

Designed by Ken Vail Graphic Design, Cambridge
Illustrations by Judith Lawton
Printed in Hong Kong / China

02 01
10 9 8 7 6 5 4 3 2

ISBN 0 431 02487 1

Some words are shown in bold, **like this**. You can find out what they mean by looking in the glossary. The glossary also helps you say difficult words.

British Library Cataloguing in Publication Data

Woodhouse, Jayne
Helen Keller. - (Lives & times)
1. Keller, Helen, 1880–1968 - Juvenile literature 2. Blind-deaf - United States - Biography - Juvenile literature
I. Title
362 .4'1'092

Acknowledgements

The Publishers would like to thank the following for permission to reproduce photographs:

American Foundation for the Blind, Helen Keller Archives: p22; Corbis-Bettmann p18; The Ronald Grant Archive p23; Chris Honeywell pp20-21; Perkins School for the Blind, Massachusetts p19

Cover photograph reproduced with permission of Hulton Getty.

Every effort has been made to contact copyright holders of any material reproduced in this book. Any omissions will be rectified in subsequent printings if notice is given to the Publisher.

Helen tried to learn about the world
around her. She used her **sense** of touch
and her sense of smell.

A wild child

Because Helen could not hear, she did not know how to talk. She made up her own signs. If she wanted an ice cream she shivered!

There were many things Helen could not understand. This made her very angry and she kicked and screamed.

A famous friend

'That child is stupid!' said Helen's uncle.
'You must send her away!'
'No,' replied her mother, 'we must find a
way to help her.'

In those days, no one knew how to help children who were **deaf** and **blind**. Her parents took Helen to see **Dr Alexander Graham Bell**. He helped them find a teacher for Helen.

A teacher

When Helen was six years old her teacher arrived. First, Annie Sullivan had to make Helen do as she was told. One day she spent two hours making Helen eat with a spoon and not her hand!

Soon Helen began to trust Annie and
obey her. All the time, Annie was
tracing letters into Helen's hand. But
Helen did not understand that d-o-g
meant dog, or d-o-l-l meant doll.

A little miracle

Then one day Annie put Helen's hand under the water pump. In her other hand she **traced** w-a-t-e-r. Suddenly Helen understood that water was the name of the cool thing running over her hand.

Now Helen began to learn very fast.
Soon she knew hundreds of words. She
learnt to read and write **braille**.

Learning to speak

Helen wanted to speak. She learned by touching her teacher's lips or tongue and copying the movements. She was soon able to make the different sounds.

Still Helen wanted to learn more. She went to **university**. Annie was always with her. Annie had to read all the books for Helen and **trace** the words into her hand.

Telling the world

Helen spent the rest of her life helping others with special needs. She raised lots of money for **blind** people.

Helen wrote a lot and travelled all over the world to give **lectures**. She wanted to show what **deaf** and blind people could do. She died in 1968 when she was 87.

Photographs

Because Helen was a famous person,
there are many photographs of her.
Here she is at 17 years old, with
Annie Sullivan.

This is Helen again, at the age of 80. She is reading one of her **braille** books. Can you see the dots?

Books

When Helen was 22, she wrote her **autobiography**. In the book she tells us what it felt like to be **deaf** and **blind**.

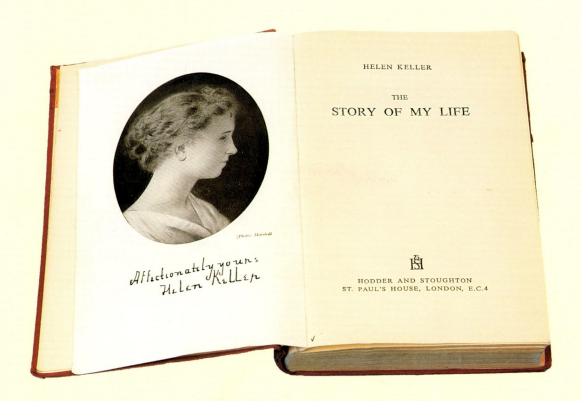

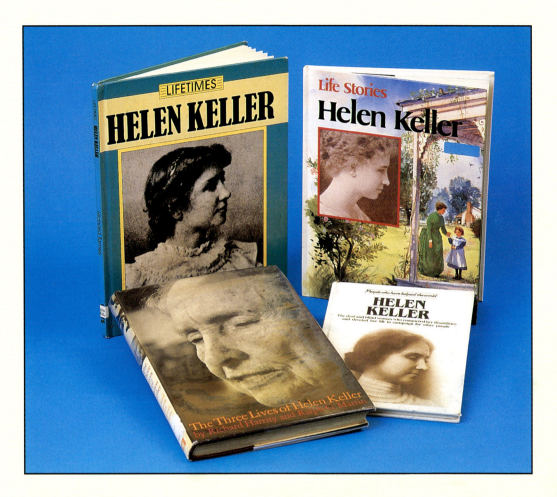

Many **authors** have also written books about Helen Keller. Some are for adults and some are for children. There may be some in your local library.

Buildings

The house in America where Helen Keller grew up is now a **museum**. Inside you can see the room where she was born.

Films

A film was made about Helen's life. It is called *The Miracle Worker*. Although it was made a long time ago, it is still shown on television.

Glossary

This glossary explains difficult words, and helps you to say words which are hard to say.

author a person who writes books. You say *or-ther*

autobiography a book written by someone about his or her own life. You say *or-toe-bi-og-ra-fee*

blind not able to see

braille a special kind of writing with dots that you feel, for the blind to read, invented by Louis Braille. You say *brale*

deaf not able to hear

Dr Alexander Graham Bell the inventor of the telephone. He also knew how to help deaf people because his mother and wife were both deaf.

lectures a talk given to group of people to teach them about something. You say *lek-chers*

museum a building which contains objects that tell us about how people lived or worked in the past

obey do as you are told. You say *o-bay*

sense how you know about things around you, your body has five senses: smell, touch, sight, hearing and taste

tracing using the finger to write letters. You say *tray-sing*

university a place to go on to for more study, after you have finished school

Index